Staple 50

TWENTY YEARS
OF
TWENTIETH CENTURY
POETRY

EDITED BY
Donald Measham and Bob Windsor
DESIGN BY
Bill Berrett

Spring 2001

Staple
20 YEARS OF TWENTIETH
CENTURY
POETRY
Donald Measham
&
Bob Windsor

ISBN 1 901185 02 8
©
Individual Contributors
2001
©
(This Selection)
Measham/Windsor 2001

Staple 50
ISSN 0266 - 4410

TYPESET
by
Roger Booth Associates
Hassocks, West Sussex
in
Palatino

PRINTED
at the
Arc & Throstle Press
Nanholme Mill
Todmorden

Staple
Tor Cottage
81 Cavendish Road
Matlock Derbyshire
DE4 3HD

CONTENTS

Foreword		5
Mother Tongue	Donna Hilbert	7
Ex Libris	Elizabeth Gowing	8
Tonguings	Margaret Moore	9
Those Yearning Years	Roshan Doug	10
Sleeping In Eng Lit	Pauline Keith	11
Jonesey's War	Maurice Rutherford	12
On Bright Days Like This	Michael Daugherty	13
Vietnam	Michael Stone	14
Out With The Mole Cropper	Paul Christmas	17
Herr Friseur	Anne Kind	19
For Viola	Ulf Goebel	20
Pinochet's Hell	Sheila Hamilton	22
Order Of The Day	Ben Wilensky	23
Scilly Fools 1707	Victor Callaghan	24
Low Tide	Berenice Moore	25
Water	D A Prince	26
Equipped For Seas	Richard Epstein	27
The Levels	Jon Silkin	28
Wood Cove	Jenny King	29
Arcadia	Philip Brown	30
Walking On The Backs of Animals	Hillel Schwartz	31
'On What Branch Does Truth Blossom?'	June Ella Harris	32
Tetragrammaton	Geoff Pickering	32
Padua	Donald Measham	33
Child At Handel's *Messiah*	Pat Buik	33
The Lady And The Hare	Pauline Stainer	34
The Round	Peter Cash	35
Godchild	K V Skene	36
Catstones	Roger Elkin	36
At Tegg's Nose Quarry, Macclesfield	Maggie Norton	38
Two Observations Near Rosewell, Midlothian	Roy Blackman	39
From Thatcher In Hell	Guy Russell	40
Lines For The Miners	Paul Heapy	42
Crossing The Line	Elizabeth Barrett	42
Autobiographical	Tony Rees	44
Allotments	Roger Waterfield	45
Cari Spazzini	Julian Stannard	45
A Foot In Academe	Helen Hills	46
Ugandan Hill Women	Bob Windsor	48
A Breath Of Night Air	Caroline Price	49
At Mrs Whittaker's Canal Street	Emma Gleadall	50

Purdah	Victoria Field	51
I've Always Wanted A Cowboy	Virginia Warbey	52
Something Aunt Rosie Said	Frances Nagle	53
My Husband's Hands	Margret Christie	54
Not Queen But Pawn	Jenny Hamlett	56
Rebound	Anna Woodford	57
Electric Impulses	Barbara Daniels	58
For Jane	Eric Jones	58
Web	Berlie Doherty	60
Rydal Water	John Sewell	61
Cow	Ann Atkinson	62
Hand Washing A Smock	Mary Maher	63
Pavement Artist	Michael Henry	64
Round	Jill Young	65
Taking Mark This Time	Tim Love	66
Culling The Herd	Jennifer Olds	67
Haunting	Janet Loverseed	68
How He Will Remember Me	Claudette Bass	68
Over And Over With Affection	Jim Lockley	70
Partners	Bob Cooper	70
The Roberts	Paddy Kitchen	71
Sunday School Outing To The Bluebell Woods	Frances Wilson	72
Portrait After Kandinsky	John Ringrose	73
Meat	Tobias Hill	74
Fallen Fruit	Ursula Kiernan	75
Dancing Attendance	Keith Ashton	76
Some Things That Go To Make A Golden Wedding	Keith Ashton	77
The Midges	James Brockway	78
Thin Air	Diana Syder	79
One Flesh	Julia Casterton	79
In G Major	Huw Watkins	80
Dear Second Bed Down	Geoffrey Holloway	81
Your Country	Patricia Pogson	81
Crypt	Catherine Byron	82
Prayer	Eamer O'Keeffe	83
Fat Shadow	David Duncombe	84
Skinning The Bull	John Daniel	85
Leading Marigold To The Bull	Chris Maudsley	86
Dog	William Imray	87
Road Kill: On Seeing A Dead Cat Freed From Winter's Icy Grip	Michael-J Bakerpearce	88
Contributors		89
Photograph and Credits		96

FOREWORD

Writer's workshops at Matlock began as long ago as 1971. They became regular events attended by poets from as far away as Southampton. They also gave rise to Staple magazine, which has over two decades published two and a half thousand poems. Eighty of them are gathered in the present publication.

It would be as true to say (for all our editorial care) that the poems chose themselves as that we did the choosing. They are non-metropolitan, open but un-cool, free from evasion, not mannered, traditional but unhackneyed. If they hold together and stand the test of time, it is perhaps because they were never fashionable. Their medium is, as Wordsworth had it, 'a selection of the real language of [women] and men in a state of vivid sensation.'

The poems come from New York, California, Canada, and from Highland Scotland to Cornwall via the Isle of Man and Wales; and there is an off-centre, almost a regional feel about them. To say so is not faint praise or disavowal. On the contrary, when one recalls the place of the regions in twentieth century English poetry: from Lawrence to Auden, from Hughes, Harrison and Larkin, from Douglas Dunn to R S Thomas, from Bunting and Nicholson to, say, Geoffrey Hill – and to Roy Fisher, who had a hand in the founding of Staple...

Every effort has been made to contact the authors or their representatives for permission to reprint their Staple poems in this fiftieth issue. Our apologies to anyone whom we have been unable to find. Please write to us in such a case.

Donald Measham, Bob Windsor, *Matlock, Derbyshire, Spring 2001*

*

Correspondence about this Publication
To the above at Tor Cottage, 81 Cavendish Rd, Matlock, Derbyshire DE4 3HD; or, Gilderoy East, Upperwood Rd, Matlock Bath, Derbyshire DE4 3PD

All Other Business
To Ann Atkinson and Elizabeth Barrett, editors Staple 51 and after: Padley Rise, Nether Padley, Grindleford, Hope Valley, Derbyshire S32 2HE

Year of publication in Staple is given throughout.

MOTHER TONGUE

My mother tongue
unrolls along the red dirt plain:
slow, tacky,
unfolding like the dream
that catches everything.

My red mother tongue
unrolls in rows of cotton,
alfalfa, fields of wheat,
and in the green water
of the silty river.

And in the back yard
on a summer's night, in grass
thick with chiggers,
red ants, stickers.
My slick mother tongue

switches legs for talking ugly,
pitching a fit, throwing a hissy.
My slick red sticky mother tongue
can lick any little pistol,
and keeps the ring-tailed tooters

toeing the line.

Donna Hilbert   1993

EX LIBRIS

Archbishop Marsh built the extensive Marsh's Library in Dublin. Hidden in one of its 25,000 books is the letter written to him by his daughter when she eloped. It has yet to be found.

You once told me that the librarian's skill lay
in the careful choice of binding
(this as you weighed a well-thumbed favourite in your hand,
the vellum warming against your own
leathery liver-spotted skin).

You showed me all the tricks of that trade,
the pummelling of the hide of calves,
its dimpling under the brusque dark inky stamp
of an insistent press,
the lick of the illuminator's soft-curled brush
gilded with rare liquids.
You showed me how to hoard the beauties carefully
until a young man with the right credentials came,
hungry for knowledge.
Then you would loose one book a chain's length
and leave them alone together
in the musky quiet.
Sometimes you stood –
I saw you –
breathing carefully just outside the bays
to watch the expectant scholar
cradling or stroking an exquisite spine,
bent to hear the soft whispering
of the pages.
And when the silent men had taken what they wanted
and had gone,
you darted in yourself
to check for chapters ripped or stained,
needing to feel them all your own again,
inhaling their animal smell
with your animal smile.

Of course I left you.
I explained it in my letter
and to find it you will have to frisk
each of your twenty five thousand darlings,
checking their secret places
before you come
to the book with a broken binding,
gilt-edged.

Elizabeth Gowing   2000

TONGUINGS

Day after day you *filled in my far fields*
with home-baked commendations.
There were times, even so, with you at the end of your tether,
when I felt the rough edge of older Derry tongues.

As when you caught me, *both arms the one length*,
with a table to clear and a bedroom *like Paddy's market*,
or when I'd weighed down your purse with *fiddler's money*.

Those were the worst of times to admit defeat:
The old dog for the hard road!
Or present petitions:
Let him go and snuff peat!
Or misplace a schoolbook:
You'll be chasing the crows for that one day!
A voice from the famine, surely?

Yet every once in a while your ghosts were genial:
The man who never made a mistake never made anything.
And later, when I first talked about crossing the water,
You've a free foot and a fellow for it.
At hours when other words fail I savour that lilting lie.

Margaret Moore   2000

THOSE YEARNING YEARS

Upon his face I saw for years as he printed Urdu
strokes about going back when the kids have grown.

And then I'd scribble a foreign name and write
a familiar phrase 'wife of' or 'son of' followed by an inky

tribal surname, corrupted by the snow and the rain.
At times I posted those letters light as the Indian

Ocean to which I directed them. And my father
would explain the family tree how we all fitted in

and tell me who was who and in which village he lived
pride and passion in his voice and a yearning to go back

home. And I'd imagine a far away world like Timbuktu
where a man's status was defined by the number of

buffaloes he had or acres under his name, not by
a simple degree from an odd university, locked away

in a drawer made of English Oak, an acknowledgement
rarely made, but an embarrassment all the same.

Roshan Doug   1998

SLEEPING IN ENG LIT

'You mean you let him sleep?'
'No point in waking him. He was dog-tired.'
            'But in your lesson!'
Her eyes don't yet reflect
that I am pleased.
                    That class
have let me in. We slam the door
on seethings, apathy, explosions
– all the negatives of School –
policed by the prowling Deputies.
This group has no feud that I can
feel – doesn't splinter dangerously.

There are off-days, some gloom;
blessedly, no bloody-mindedness.

So when John laid his head
on his spread arms while I
held forth on Thomas Hardy,
I'd seen his late-night eyes:
this wasn't meant to undermine.
Paul, beside him, grinned at me,
signing should he prod him. I
waved my hand to leave him be.

We talked on, over his dark hair
flopped across one hand, the other
flung to hang a little off the desk.

He looked childlike as he woke.
But his grown-up self took over,
came to murmur his regrets
as 5B moved on out.

'It's a compliment,' I told him.

(If the DES were different,
I'd like it on my reference.)

'You felt safe enough to sleep.'

Pauline Keith   1994

JONESEY'S WAR
for Selwyn Pritchard

Town Centre, Bridlington, 1994

I'm waiting at the lights, prepared to start,
side window down. A diesel lorry's fumes,
thinned in the morning air, and... / Fast Rewind
reels fifty years away and rips my mind
off weekend shopping lists; a gut-pang zooms
me overseas, back to that tank, at night
in laager, half an hour before first light
or, as we used to call it, sparrowfart...

> **Together we'll hit the enemy for six, right out of Africa**
> *– Montgomery to the Eighth Army, El Alamein, 1942*

But some who didn't make it,
bowled cheaply out, Jonesey saw once more
commemorated in the Officers' Store at Base,
their monument of hat-boxes, polo-sticks,
tin trunks stencilled with kite-strings
of initials like the Gentlemen
versus Players list. He heard again
their short-tongued talk of meets
and varsities soon taken up by others
fresh from home, 'the Nigels, Claudes
and Francises and Something-Fucking-Smiths'.
(It was Jonesey when his gearbox jammed
came on the intercom, 'Oh, fuck!
The fucking fucker's fucking fucked!
Fucking fuck it!', then coaxed it cursing
twenty sandstorm miles to Bir Hakeim.)

But bloody officer chaps! A breed apart.
Take Jonesey's tank commander, Punjab Payne.
'Doolally, him! And regi-fucking-mental?
Put *himself* on a charge one time:
"Whilst On Active Service, as Officer Of The Day,
I failed to visit the Men's Mess-tent at Tiffin."
Cupid stunt – too much fucking desert sun!
Ambition, "To be killed in action, then father
would just *have* to be proud of me."
Fuck that for a game of soldiers!
While fucking Jonesey's driving this tank
he's not going to get *us* all killed.'

And no, he didn't. Punjab took solace –
an MC when the gongs came up
the sharp end, with the rations.
Jonesey? 'Mentioned In Fucking Dispatches.'
Carried a crafty bat and came back home
to 'slog the lisping bastards out of sight
with Clement-Fucking-Attlee'.

...I'm sitting at the *Sherman's* wireless set,
been on the air since sparrowfart searching
the band; my call-sign comes, I lock on net.
Engines warmed up, guns proved, fresh char brewing...
Loud hooting and the green above me calls
for action: handbrake, clutch – my *Escort* stalls,
and while the amber light gives way to red
half Bridlington looks on. I stare ahead
as – is it Jonesey? – from the fumes behind:
'You fucking deaf? – as well as fucking blind?'

Maurice Rutherford   1994

ON BRIGHT DAYS LIKE THIS

On bright days like this, when the sun
blesses my survival, runs an understanding
finger over the jigsaw puzzle
of my skull, I can forget the demands
of disfigurement, relax
in my patched flesh.

On my own front step to perhaps
a fuller recovery than the surgeon guessed,
I am safe from passers-by,
their snide asides and snipers' eyes,
free to hold my head high
above any need to hide
the bullet-hole of simply
a neat extra dimple.

The weather has never
been cleverer.

Michael Daugherty   1992

VIETNAM

Show it to me on the map! And you say
This slender funnel, this river-fluted
Tuber grown out of the Chinese potato
Today contaminates the good food we eat?

In Europe time is running out – in Vietnam
Time – history's fuse – is burning
From both sides towards the centre.

Only because Auden is silent, the skin
Of his face like vellum upon which are recorded
The battles lost and a multitude of honours;

Only because Brecht is dead and Hikmet
Lies buried in a Moscow cemetery, only because
Neruda appears to be growing too fond of flowers;

Only because the aesthetics of statistics demand
A harmony of casualties, the equipoise of havoc:
So many small brown bodies as against

So many tall ones, either pink or black –
All of theme lifeless; so many huts destroyed
As against a jet's intricate wreckage;

So many villages utterly pacified
By the obscene fruits of patient research;
So much metal and muscle abused

In the foolish endeavour to pervert a people's
Factual prayers; so much jungle
Despoiled and so many reclaimed by the jungle ...

Only because we may still stand upright, while they
Must crouch in their burrows or pretend compliance
With the law of the gas-shell and the whore's surrender;

Only because those not yet born one day
Will look at us with puzzled eyes or pityingly:
Who've built aerials sensitive to the first faint greeting

From the most distant stars, yet lack the antennae
To pick up the whimpers of our labouring earth:
Pangs of a new genesis conceived in the years

When suffrage was hoisting its flag of smoke
Atop the first factory chimney and the women huddled
Together of a cold morning in the first loom-shed ...

Because of all this and because each far from
Miraculous birth, however untimely
Or however discourteous to the lugubrious forecasters ...

Just when the bidding is at its highest, let's say,
At Sotheby's for an ancient manuscript proclaiming
(Though this is not the reason for its record price):

'Though art born free, O Man! Thou shalt
Cherish thine freedom and at all times defend it
Even as a lioness defends her cubs', or

Disrupting a conference of the five or six bankers
Whose aloof decisions may mean death or dance,
Or in the middle of a sermon exhorting us to be patient ...

Is as a new fountain suddenly sprung up
From among the rocks, as a sprig of parsley
Joyously discovered in the waste land,

We must school ourselves in a midwife's skills,
Take up the arms of the learned obstetrician
To foil history's abortionists; pitting

Against their pure love of power, their idol rights
Of thin blood and fat portfolios,
The surpassing power of our impure loves.

Allons, Vietcong! Who thought to poison your trees
Thereby loosened their seedpods: Now they drift
Across Asia to the fertile soil of London's parks.

Allons, Vietcong! Who relied on burning your crops
Forgot the contagion from empty drums: Now the favelas
of Rio are humming, the shanties around Jo'burg.

Allons, Vietcong! Who hoped with tawdry to buy
The love of even the most humble of your brothers:
Now go in the fear of every whistling shoeblack.

Only because their scientists must retrace the years
Of learning for the one vital mistake, the hidden crack
In the foundations; only because their philosophers

Are busy procuring new euphemisms for the inadmissible
Defeat; only because their generals now wish
Theirs had been the career of the first- or second-born,

As banking and diplomacy do not have to contend with
So unfathomable a factor as a man's stubborn vision;
Only because the buds of our most tender hopes
are proving too spiky for even the hawks' crooked beaks:

Let me show it to you on the map! I say
This slender funnel, this river-fluted
Tuber grown out of the Chinese potato
Today is preparing the good food we'll eat tomorrow!

In Europe time may be running out – In Vietnam
Time – History's fuse – is burning
From both sides towards the centre.

Michael Stone   1984*

* Michael Stone wrote *Vietnam* in German, his first language. It was published in Berlin in the 1960s. The Staple text is his own previously unpublished English version.

OUT WITH THE MOLE CROPPER

I

When you pulled one from the gallery
and dusted down your sleeve
earth still clung to your face and fell from its.
Dark blemishes easily brushed away.
You laid it down, elegant in its death
perfectly shaped, not at all like a discarded glove.
The day smelled ordinary.

I remember the time you had shown me
how to scrape away the heave of soil;
you pitched your hand into the tunnel
and pulled out a ball of moss and leaves
which you broke to let light fall
onto the four furless young.
I watched them squirm like grubs, decocooned
and failed to persuade you to replant them.
I knew that they would not return to grow blue pelts.

The traps still hang on the gable end
ten or a dozen attached by nail and twine;
cold fingers designed to grip those that blindly
nudged and ruzzled the wrong route;
those larvae devouring scraps of miniature darkness.

And you, the cropper, would tug blue fruit from the soil.

At the click of a knife outsize hands,
that twitched and flicked, dropped to earth
before the blade's dash from vent to vent,
then the flesh rolled away.
How easy the separation;
how quick the return to a grotesque and naked youth.

And always you would say, 'Lady let me take your coat.'

II

It's easier now, the heavy gas curls along passageways
to fill their silent rooms. They are too slow to heed
the blue touch-paper warning, just a ruler down.
Waiting dogs refuse the cores evicted from their skins.
I take a spade and turn them in, turn them in.

III

She thumbed them,
turned each like a compass to find their east and west.

Then, once arranged she joined four
so their edges brushed
like strangers in a gallery.

Her fingers ran along them
forming faint grey ghosts in the pile.

A small, ornamental cap covered the crown of her hair.
Her black dress like a priest's cassock
with its row of black bone buttons
told the locals that
she was not of this place.
'Perhaps darkness comes cheap today,'
filtered out through knuckles
pressed close to dialect lips.

While she rolled one
six by four over outstretched fingers,
and collared part of her hand,
returning flesh to the skin's interior,
a light rain fell on the skylight
and regulars turned away
preferring other stalls with more edible fare.

She seemed qualified in skin.

Somewhere, I thought, there must be
a Mordecai, Jacob or Ezra
that would invite her in,
consider her judgements,
the quality of her skins.
Where they were and what they did
with these blue pelts
that once had grubbed in soil
people only guessed at.

She collected them from the trestle top
unbuttoned her coat and placed each one,
the pin side of her turquoise brooch,
into the dark and silent room of an inner pocket.

Soon she would, like the others, collect her children
and be forced to board the train,
filled with those who would curl in gas
to be robbed of their skins through which light would pass.
There is no bargaining when you arrive
to prevent the scalpel's cold insertion
which will inch its way till it finds release.
Lady, button up, hold tightly to your coat.

Paul Christmas   1998

HERR FRISEUR

I thought you would always be there
Cutting and waving Mutti's hair

I remember you tall, blue eyed, fair
You kept her secret to the end.

Sent us away to play so you could get on
With what had to be done behind closed doors.

Once, when your back was turned I peeped
Saw her wearing a curious black cape for dying hair.

What happened to you Herr Friseur, did you shave
Innocent heads?
Who paid for that public service?

Anne Kind   1990

FOR VIOLA

*On 6 July 1994 Pope John Paul II honored Kurt Waldheim,
the former President of Austria and Secretary-General of
the United Nations who had been an intelligence officer
attached to units of the Wehrmacht involved in atrocities,
by making him a knight of the Ordino Piano.*

I cannot think it.
I cannot think Waldheim's
being knighted
by the current Pope

for efforts of peace
and humanitarian
activities in the service
of the United Nations.
I cannot understand,
cannot accept,

the concomitant
lack of distress,
lack of sorrow.
My father rounded up Jews.
My father served on the Eastern Front.
My father attained a rank
similar to Waldheim's, with decorations
of equal import. I can only

say he should be knighted
as well, in all fairness,
posthumously, for all he might have
done, had he lived, like Waldheim.
Like Waldheim he would have
said it was time to put things

behind us. I cannot
do the unimaginable,
cannot fall, like the sunlight
in a photograph I have seen,
through the trees at the edge
of a wood, alongside
the road curving out from among them,
into the patch of grass sharply

in focus between the naked, atrophied
thighs of a young woman. Her one
leg is slightly drawn up, the foot
still wearing its shoe, the stocking awry
at the ankle. The other is completely
bare, the leg stretched out, the skirt
twisted up at the waist. To both sides

of the still, pale, delicately shadowed bowl
of her abdomen, defining it, the immaculate

points of bone. She must have been dragged
to lie among the rest of the thousands
of corpses awaiting transport. I can imagine

nothing I might say, nothing
like achieving in the black
and white surface of silver
chlorides, bromides, halides, iodides,
or whatever may have been fixed
in the emulsion, now the printer's
mere ink of reproduction, a kind

of breeze to stir the blades etched there,
if only that, to brush a little
over those feelingless, emaciated, youthful
planes of nakedness, those alabaster
projections of fragility, that dark texture
of perfection harboring no further

enticements to anyone of her own kind.
What is the use of this? The wooded
landscape may have changed little
since the Day of Liberation. Others
have made their home here. The Church

has spoken. It never happened.
To say so, benighted,
is to leave no room for human error.

Ulf Goebel   1995

PINOCHET'S HELL

So let's suppose it's true,
that each of us makes
our own, particular hell.

Imagine Pinochet's.
His soul transported
to the ditches of the sea
where they dumped the tortured corpses,

believing, as one would, that they'd break up.
They didn't,
They transformed,
quickly adapting to the taste of salt.

And here they are:
puffer-fish arching and flexing their spikes,
blood-coloured octopus curling their legs,
legs that look like ropes,

and an entire army of the species *Holothuria* –
trepangs, beches-de-mer, – advancing,
to squirt not ink but their own intestines,
then growing some more, to squirt again,

and, also, eels,
thicker than pythons, almost smiling
as they send their shocks.
Spotting him, they turn up the voltage.

Sheila Hamilton   2000

ORDER OF THE DAY

It is the order of the day to be taunted by the sea,
anointed by a hurricane with a sense of humor.
In the time it takes for a line to snap,
or a single bird to fly the coop,
great armadas disappear, go down.
Haunted by this mal de mer,
we pray to God to interfere before we drown.

On a dead calm night when my watch was still,
a massive wave slammed my hull and sliced through steel
the way a butcher guts his cow.
There were screams and noise of men and boys,
legs, limbs, floating on the outward tide.
Dazed by the fury of this shark attack,
I lost my ability to play, to be resilient in this century.
I became homeless and numb, a refugee.

When least expected, least demanded,
least believed in anything at all,
peace resumed on Friday.
In front of my nose in a provocative pose
was a Great Blue Whale sunning her body,
singing a song lasting ten minutes long
of twisting parody,
believable simplicity.

Her gown was made of barnacles and shells,
skin more beautiful than gold,
and when she breached,
she reached into the sky.
In the time it takes for clouds to rain,
or a fool to piss away his pain,
her calf was born.
It is the order of the day to be amazed,
to be torn
in two.

Ben Wilensky   2000

SCILLY FOOLS 1707

Seamen who call a spade a spade
would call Shovell a shit –
Admiral Sir Cloudesley Shovell:
no other word's so fit.

He's leading the line up-Channel
miles off-course in a fog,
relying on dead-reckoning
with the old line and log,

when up pipes one seasoned seaman
too troubled to hold his tongue –
he wants to warn the Admiral
his navigation's wrong…

Well, the Navy calls that mutiny,
so without more ado
the poor chap's hoisted like a flag –
a signal to the crew.

Pour encourager les autres
his feet don't touch the deck:
he's swinging from a yardarm with
a rope around his neck.

So four ships run on Gilstone Rocks
and split and go straight down –
taking with them two thousand men:
only two don't drown.

Of course one is their Admiral:
he won't go down – no fear!
Let them go to hell – he can swim:
the coast could be quite near…

Yes: he's washed up on St Mary's,
spreadeagled on the shore –
but then a beachcomber comes along
and settles Shovell's score.

She can't miss the great emerald
glistening on his hand:
decides she'll have that – and the rest,
so fills his face with sand.

You could call that dead reckoning –
two ways to suffocate:
letting your tongue wag, flashing your ring –
two ways of tempting fate.

Victor Callaghan   1999

LOW TIDE

Today the sea has poured itself away
over the edge of the world
leaving the wide, wet flats empty
for the sun and sky to play with.

The sun has performed its usual magic:
soft, wet slush to particles of light,
brown and bronze and buff and beige
and blue where the sky has fallen
into the lows and shallows.

We walk on the shining floor of the sea
following the waters
out and on to Ultima Thule
to be lost in the mist and thunder
of the ever-falling water.

Berenice Moore   1998

WATER

Runs in the family, my father says
plumbing the rough hedge, deep
in hawthorn, bramble, till his hands
recognise the fit of hazel. One slice
with the knife I'm never allowed to touch
and it's sprung, his trap
for mapping springs, and their secret
underground channellings.

He'd picked it up,
its twisted fluent tongue,
easy as speech, his father's trade,
born to bricks, native bonds,
building of wells; skills like mixing mortar,
levelling, sealing off – and took for granted
the hazel's blunt spur, dipping and rearing,
compelled by liquid signals.
Codes of water, translated
down Plynlimon's rusty torrents and sour rushes,
slipping into thin soil, through shale;
an inevitable geography.
Perhaps the day he learned was like today:
late May, young lambs now clever with grass,
blackbirds as sharp as slate
scoring their songs on the blue air.

Walking this stubborn field,
stumbling, my hands closed within his, pulse to pulse,
I feel the wounded hazel buck and curve, watch
in wonder the wrenching message as it tracks
the clean lie of water, knowing something true
revealed through this: a necessary rhythm,
an inheritance.

D A Prince   2000

EQUIPPED FOR SEAS

Noah couldn't see why fish
should do so well in times of woe,
friends galore, shoals of each kind,
even schools. He heard them sing,

Hey, hey – goodbye. Noah thought his
God liked fish, liked shrimp. And krill
must have gone out nights with God,
bowling. He liked them so: saved them

from the arid death of land.
The grampus prayed. For those who go
to land in carts, their carts so small,
we pray, Oh Lord. And He was there.

He marked the fall of oysters. When
the torrents fell, flounders rejoiced;
but when the dove returned, the squid
raised eyes and arms and sent their wish,

In this the hour of return,
You cede the sand its little space,
remember us. If Noah made
his wetter moments wine, once dried,

perhaps he was remembering
the triumphs of the fins, the scales
that weighed and waited, found him not
equipped for seas, and still were there.

Richard Epstein   1997

THE LEVELS

Past Quaking Houses,
on the bull-neck of the north Pennines, that has no head,
in a flat torn sky,
wind circling among hills, like a miner
with a wide shallow bowl, panning –
above Alston, I went with my nets
to dismal grass-blobbed flats, reaching
into the Solway's firth, soft basement
to rubbed, soft water
not poisoned yet by fission, where the fish frisk
in a dismal sort of way. Their tails lash
the brunette forms of the sea.

My nets an impediment over shoulders, catching
at knees, or scraping the back of calf and thigh.
On a journey not so big as a rushlight,
the bog's rushes smeared with sheep's fat,
I went. The quaker graveyard still scythed
of nettle and its remedy, dock. At Silloth
I threw my nets into the sea,
their meshes chagrined with a dead
exposure to air, and no fish.
Nets that weighed on me, hiss in the floating sea.
For hours, against the sea's pull
tugging like any fish's mouth, green flimsy
triangles of salt wrinkling greek characters
on sifting illiterate sand.

At length six fish obliged, as if for pity
flickering over meshes they can't pass. I pulled
them out gasping against the heft
of frigid water, with biting mouths,
scraping the element they leave.
And their doleful eyes and breathless gills
tricked of their pasture hang in bodies
laid by on the denser lingual
of a muddled slap.

The silence thickens
and turns to water: lives that bite
the shining levels of mud,
the creamy monstrous air, teeth that gnash it,
are dying. Teeth and eyes hook
with a presentiment of my death.
I have taken your lives –
delicate adroit netsman.

Jon Silkin 1986

WOOD COVE

Descending steps into the narrow cove
Where a brown river mingles water with
The flatness of the sea, that salty light,
Among children loud at play I notice
A boy tumbled on pebbles, from a height.

An eye blink, a straight look: he dissolves,
Tee-shirt, hip and silent, shadowed face,
To a washed-up rag and flat, triangular stone,
While all the others, circling, larking, calling,
Jump into focus, leaving him alone.

But in that fraction of a second, snapped
Between the seeing him and the not-seeing,
Why did I feel no grief at all? Surprise,
A sort of shock – but if he had existed,
Then I betrayed him, not their carefree cries.

Does every flicker that makes up our sight
Not have validity? Like shingle? Foam?
The water-mill of knowing lets me feel.
Climbing on up the other side, I mourn
For both of us, trapped either side the real.

Jenny King 1992

ARCADIA

The landscape of Arcadia
    Can change before your eyes,
For its contours are subjective
    And its element, surprise.

The clearing in the forest
    Dissolves in summer air,
As a naiad by the lakeside
    Reveals her auburn hair;

Or the subtle surf is curling
    On the Polynesian shore,
Where coral castles waver
    Above the ocean floor;

Or outback fades to desert
    And dunes of trembling sand
Where the blue and gold horizon
    Conceals the promised land.

But isolated crofters
    Must till an arid soil,
And happy pastoral poems
    Idealise their toil,

And girls that Gauguin painted
    Have different goods to sell,
For sweet Miranda's island
    Housed Caliban as well,

And the boy who trod the songlines
    And became the exiles' guide
Contracted their infection,
    Lay down, and quietly died.

So that we should surrender
    Our wish to travel there,
Relinquish to Arcadia
    Its thin untroubled air,

And keep within a country
    Whose borders are confined,
And leave intact for ever
    These Edens of the mind.

Philip Brown   1997

WALKING ON THE BACKS OF ANIMALS

I am walking from Moonlight to Stone
Steps on the backs of animals, one after another
kneeling in cold waters at low tide,
still as monks, heads bent under cowls or rounded off or lost
to salt: deer, antelope, bison, boar
dazed by arctic winds and winter storm, naked of their sand
from haunch to ridge of spine, sea
cows, great black labradors – Peaceable Kingdom of backs
to take me safe in my forty-odd years
from middle earth past middle age to middle school,
something ever to jump across: a spell,
a times, a long division, a grandma's back, and here I am
alone, far too proud of unbroken bones,
leaping from ram to panther, elk to lion, when it's luck
and rough weather that brings me
to this land's end of cliffs and ancient patient animals
holding their breath as I pass
over, one sure foot upon one dark unmoving back
and then another, miles up the coast,
from hippo to rhino to tortoise all the way back
but not quite home.

Hillel Schwartz   1996

'ON WHAT BRANCH DOES TRUTH BLOSSOM?'
Mandelstam

And how he swore
her lies were true

And how she drew
the branches down

And how he loved
her even then

And how she pared
his skin to bone

And how he kept
her fragrance close

Until she broke
the blossom's crown

June Ella Harris   1992

TETRAGRAMMATON

To the ancient Hebrews, God was a four-letter word
Like ✶✶✶✶ or ———
Too intimate to be written
Too significant to be spoken
Too close to the centre of being
No coarse vowels for the vulgar to mouth harshly

But consonants only, soft as the gasp
Of a dying saint.

Geoff Pickering   1996

PADUA

The lingua franca
of St Anthony
is on display
in the basilica

Glassplate ensures
he's no soft touch

Behind the altars
stone is bulled like a boot
as handling weepers
detect inset reliquaries

The boards
(lodged in the university)
from which Galileo gave tongue
lack polish
Still have a rough edge

Donald Measham   1984

CHILD AT HANDEL'S *MESSIAH*

Sleeps in his African grandmother's lap
sound as a drunk, as drunk he is
on the bottle of milk she fed to him
before the start. His curly head
is peeping out like a black lamb
between his hood and the crook of her arm.
And when he stirs, she sways her knees
and later shifts his head to the other
side, so then it's green and ruby
trousers, little dangling feet
in black lacing shoes that charm
the row behind, impressed by her
and the quiet child. So cradled by sound
'Hallelujah, Hallelujah!'
he sleeps on through Glory to God
feeding his flock, and his yoke is easy.

Pat Buik   1999

THE LADY AND THE HARE

They would have your believe
she slept on bedrock
where ash roots the stone

that what startled silence
was not a buzzard mewing
but the huntsman's horn unblown.

When the hounds
broke from their thicket
they froze at her calm

sensed in the cold apse
of her breast
both the dove and the bone.

Today we started no hare;
downstream of the waterfall
found only her shrine

and how sternly
the warm hare is folded
inside her fierce gown.

Pauline Stainer   1992

THE ROUND

Farm-lights show through the poplars.
Delivering orders, Dad and I drive
off the pre-fabricated estate
into open country ... The moon

sits boat-wise in black water-sky.
Hares move among the fodder:
as our Ford van runs on the rim
of a silver dyke, I see them leap

round unconcerned cattle, their lugs
flickering ... 'Damn nuisances!' says Dad.
What am I to think? a mere boy raised
where men earn meagre livings

decapitating cabbage-fields
and Marshall's lorries mud the road.
We leave another tight-packed box
redolent of *Omo* and *Typhoo*:

'Hares in yon field,' my father says.
(... 'With tender moonlit ears,' I add,
let into their deep-secret life).
'Damn things!' agrees the wife.

Peter Cash   1996
             Friskney 1961

GODCHILD

```
We went down together, slipped
through the eye of the needle,
back-doored out of the garden,
cut loose       no one wants        a god
our god            or sees          damn trick
you                   now           can never set us free
keep us            my god           from our death
in mirrors     we grow mad          child
as an unrepentant poet, bitchy
as a witch in heat – slowburn
from your unself-centred eye.
```

K V Skene   1994

CATSTONES

I

Laze in the sun, stretching their lengths,
Asserting their presence
For weather's fingerings.

To most they're just another pile of rocks
In a landscape packed with rocks,
Outcrop islands, heaps of boulders, stones, peaks, crags –
Almost boring in their persistence.

To those privy to moor's secrets
They're known as part Bronze Age Fort
Dedicated to the celebration of the Cat.

(Strange how names remain, while history's forgot.)

II

Our nine cats have answered their summons
As magicking, the rocks have dragged them
Magneting to the north.
Each cat in turn suddenly stupid,
Entranced, then transfixed by the soundless song.

Each cat, in turn,
Deaf to the road's warning,
The gravel's hiss, the camber's rumble.

Each cat, in turn, found stunned, then dead.
Each limb perfect, all of it perfect,
Except the head a-tilt.

That's how they want them:
Untouched, unblemished.
Having possessed their minds,
Want completion with their limbs.

It's payment for shaping my garden
Out of moor's ground:
Their shallow graves, atonement.

What comes out, must be replaced:
Bones for stones.

Now the garden's done,
And we have no need for digging stone,
We resist requests to take more cats:

You can pay over the odds.

Roger Elkin   1993

AT TEGG'S NOSE QUARRY, MACCLESFIELD

    Look at this. I cleeve it
and it rives in two
new as a bairn's bottom
never had daylight
for millions of years.
    It were a river of muddy sand
crushed by its weight
into this bonny beauty.

    Good stuff's pink as bacon
a rough buff pink
crisp as crackling
lovely to handle and work.
    Shale's bloody useless
and that's up at top under sod.
Best grit's deep in bowels
hard work to get.

    We made all manner of things.
Slopstones and paving flags
drain holes, mill stones
roof slates, grave stones
gate posts and kerb sets.
    Yon dry stone wall
has a gritstone lintel
set above the sheep hole.
See there? I used to sharpen knives
for me mother on that grindstone.

    What's that you say?
Speak up, I'm deaf with workings.
You thought grit were sandy green?
Nay, that's weathered, weathered.
    True grit is pink.
Feel it, and tongue it,
work it and you'd understand cold.
We drill a hole, hammer in
two metal feathers and a plug
and the stone rives off.

A crowbar helps, and then
a chisel splits it open.
We cut grooves and neaten edges.
Feel this slopstone.
Corners like the inside of your elbow,
very difficult. My work.
   To shift big slabs we used
Butters Power Driven Derrick Crane,
and Jaw Crusher riddled
roadstone out of waste.

   Now sithee, behind this hut,
see this stone, it's mine.
Can you read? I carved that before the War.
It says 'Here lies Jesseth Macabody, quarryman,
born 1914, died 19 summat.'
   I told 'em I want to carve last two figures.
They promised that I can,
so I come up every day
just in case, just in case.

Maggie Norton   1993

TWO OBSERVATIONS NEAR ROSEWELL, MIDLOTHIAN

In the old days this farm would have had a horse-drawn gin.
The horse would have worked its circle for hour after hour,
turning the horizontal wheel to power
threshers, winnowers, dockers, shearers, churns.

Now it's a stud farm. The horse is still tied to the gin,
a thing like a flimsy overgrown playground roundabout,
but power is fed to a central motor to spin
it slowly, walking the racehorse as it turns.

Nearby, two men, in an open-cast coalmine, with brooms.
When the last ochre layer is scraped off and dumped in the tipper
they brush the black underlay clean, for the waiting ripper.
A village of miners reduced to two road-sweepers; grooms.

Roy Blackman   1994

From THATCHER IN HELL

She died. Her soul fled moaning to the shades
Where hatred grins, greed winks and fear pervades
So not much difference really. It was good
To meet old comrades in the neighbourhood:
Here Aitken, splayed and tortured with a baton
There Clark, hung in a sewer being shat on...
Both men had made infernal pacts before;
But she, while burning, burned to make some more.
Thinking, 'We need to get our views across',
She boldly crawled to see her Hellish boss.

'Lord Satan,' wiled the minx. 'You chair the Board.
You run the kind of ship I like, my Lord.
Efficient, unaccountable, unfair,
Your management is much admired *up there*.
(If anything, I'd say you're rather lax;
You need a carrot while you torture: tax.)
But why not rationalise your personnel?
You waste, you know, fine skills down here in Hell.
And since skilled labour tends to cause mischief,
I think you'll find there's no alternative.
So despatch the best' (she made a modest cough)
'Above, to scare those bad do-gooders off.'

The Evil One had studied her CV.
He mused: she makes me think of someone... Me!
'You're right,' he grinned, 'A radical idea!
I'd say that's worth ten million souls a year.
Well done! For that, I'll give myself a rise.
And you, go up and scheme your enterprise...'

*

Good Sergeant Blair, who leads the Righteous Squad,
Is on his Vodafone, direct to God:
'Look, G, this is the action we must take:
The only way to stop her's with a stake
In newly-privatized Hell (plc)
So big we'll vote her back to purgatory.
Let's use the market to effect our aims.
It's more efficient than the state,' Blair claims.

'I know, T,' says the Lord, '(since I am God)
You humans figure I'm a useless sod:
I do let evil triumph, *laissez-faire*,
But I'm all right up here, so I don't care.
Still, intervention's 'in' now, and what's more
She's even barmier than she was before.
I don't care if she takes my Word in vain
And twists it to her purpose once again;
But I just can't *stand* her arrogant conceit:
Next thing she'll be abolishing *my* seat.
So as it's you, I'll fit a new warhead on
And get some exercise for Armageddon.'

And CRASH! God's thunderbolt, with smart-bomb range,
Misses Maggie – but hits the Stock Exchange –
And WHASH! The Market's down in Babylon!
And SMASH! The citadels of Greed are gone!

Guy Russell   1998

LINES FOR THE MINERS

Remember the Spartans, who, it is said,
having scoured the heart of its pleasure
and imitated the rock,
turned soft, wooed comfort,
allowed themselves music of a solemn sort.

Remember the Spartans knew
the world was simply a machine built to crush them,
and how they gouged at a wilful fate
from whose face they could not turn.

As they built their city and kept it
with the last resort of virtue
they looked to the future and saw
only weakness, which they cursed and craved.

And in that weakness found themselves
bereft of all weapons but
hard love and monolithic hate.

Paul Heapy   1984

CROSSING THE LINE

Between bedsits and grant cheques
I went back to stay for free
with Dad that summer,
forced by need but lured as well
by pictures on the London Evening News;
faces pitching and jeering on the slag heaps
above Orgreave Farm where, as a child,
I'd ridden the ponies out – the familiar arcs
of white horse breath dispersing, now,
in a charge of hooves trained to centre,
the seethe and shove of crowd collapsing
beneath their riders' centrifugal swing.

I remember the north-faced house felt cold
that summer; Dad spun his coal, doled
daily quotas to the hod, while I stretched
fingers and toes to the window's light,
paused to stamp and blow between drafts
of a chapter for my PhD on class identity –
ignorant, for all that, of the way Dad's
second mortgage payments were slipping back;
not clever enough to understand what it meant
when men came to the house that day;
or work out why Dad ushered them quickly in,
closed the sitting room door on me.

And then, one morning, the manic clank
of a hammer ricocheting between brass bells,
battering me awake at 4am; my brief caught-breath
as habit counted out the clock's unwind-to-silence;
the unexpected speed of it, as if his hand waited.
Then gasp of the cold splashing; ritual creak and stir
of him dressing; single boil of the kettle; background rustle
of the greaseproof wrapping of his snap –
the clunk of lock behind him, inevitable.
Outside, low voices broke the lull; their mumbled
greetings strained, unfamiliar. I sat up, peered out
at a white van edging slowly into the mist. Slept again.

Woke imagining it all a dream. But there was this:
a policeman, outside, posted on the drive,
shifting his feet, staring out across suburban quiet;
the single brick which hit the glass behind his back.
When Dad got home he couldn't cope anymore:
could face the crowd but not his daughter's
rhetoric: *I don't have to live with this* he'd said.
Turned me out. I remember how I cried,
long months after, when they announced it over;
felt fossiled knots uncoil along my aching back.
The long fall into this well of silence had begun; the crossing
of lines that shouldn't be (the family lines I mean) irrevocably done.

Elizabeth Barrett   1999

AUTOBIOGRAPHICAL

Begin with grey, the Rhondda and the sky;
Think sodden! I remember all of it.
The colliers squatting on the pavement spit
In memory – nostalgia hurries by.
Tai school, the Empire, Porth Square, Pandy Square,
I took no time in getting out there.

They chopped off paws for fingering our farms
Those brave ghost armies on our mountainside.
Our soldiers rallied round the flags and died.
Our 'old and haughty nation, proud in arms'
Was resolute in war for every prince.
I loved to hear of that. It's gone off since.

I went and tried the proletariat then
And did my bit beside the factory gate.
The dawn would come up, tediously and late,
My papers shouted Fight! at working men
Who puffed their fags and coughed their morning cough.
'You'll buy a paper, mate?'
                    'You bugger off!'

As everyone predicted, old and wise,
I packed in daft performances like that.
I wear a false nose now, a hopeless hat.
Wisely I contemplate the custard pies
Mature as cheese as middle age begins
Dishing out cowpats and banana skins.

Tony Rees   1984

ALLOTMENTS

What is so public and so private?
What is so treasured and derided?
A palimpsest of feudal strips,
enclosure acts and cycle clips,
flat caps, war effort, the health of the nation,
competition and cooperation.
Where could one find a richer mix?
Council by-laws and bean sticks'
skeletal sculpture, encrusted sheds
for dreaming hermit crabs, neat beds,
old buckets, rusty chicken-wire,
each plot with its wispy altar-fire.

Roger Waterfield   1997

CARI SPAZZINI

The refuse collectors strike,
13th November 1992, Genoa.

Cari spazzini, I want you to know
that as far as we're concerned you
can expect the handshake of solidarity.
We know how much the city depends

on your unglamorous cleaning up of
the streets. In fact just look
at them now. Everywhere mountains
of refuse, food for the rats, for

their families. But perhaps (strictly,
you understand, between you and us)
we could come to an agreement.
In simple terms: when no one else

is around, you come and clear
that hell-heap outside our house,
(we are, after all, clean reasonable people),
and we'll continue with that solidarity.

Julian Stannard   1995

A FOOT IN ACADEME

Ah-ha, how interesting
& as I was saying
power meeting in the corridor
power, fleeing its basis in [1]
democratic meetings held in
airless
Ah Janice could you? Coffee please
for four
speaking in the post-feminist language
of absence rupture plurality & trace [2]
now Roger said to me on the phone the other day
do you agree
oh of course
absolutely
absolutely [3]
Ha Ha Ha.

No, we wouldn't dream of excluding you
just because you are a woman
please don't be absurd [4]
after all we are [5]
just like you
now – thank you Janice –
I think maybe one thing you *didn't quite understand*
& maybe it would help if I spelt it out
oh no, I'm sure it would [6]
You see, ten years ago, that is before you were here
when you were a twinkle in your parents' eye
before, in other words, you could think or dream or spell
that's, if I may put it another way,[7]
casting about for a seed [8]
yes, even at my age Derek, ha ha ha
now Janice the papers if you please

in the top drawer [9]
Now the decoupling of sex from power
absolutely as in that paper
at the Dresden conference [10]
oh awfully good
I thought it was
my paper & Dresden not half bad [11]
and beer in the corridor
oh that's something, my dear, you might not
quite understand.

Helen Hills   1991

[1] corridors, where else?
[2] balls, of course
[3] as Frank Bergstrom has observed
[4] please don't be a woman just here
[5] playing out the old male polyester sex theory
[6] so often ambivalence traps the female subject
[7] as I argued in my paper at Lublin last year
[8] the most suitable word is phenomenological
[9] *NOT* your bottom drawer, old gal!
[10] through a radical restructuring of relations
[11] despite the theoretical impasse and the third political term

UGANDAN HILL WOMEN

How should I know them, these women
Coming in soft streams from the hills
Or melting from the road's verge
Into plantations as I dust
Them with my car? They must

Spend their lives walking; to merge
At markets, like flash pools in dips
Of hollowed ground before the day's heat;
Talking in words that lose me
Glancing with eyes that choose me
For their jests.

From head loads full as pregnant hives
They set out brittle elongated ware
Baked to the sheen of pencil leads
And these, with monstrous lengths of tuberous yam
Sketch outlines of their elsewhere lives.

Where do they go when the sun's blaze
Has parched the day's commerce to dry fronds?
Do they persist through the afternoon's white
Heat, in the shade of some flat-leaved bar
Until the evening's yellow light
Gives their long march relief?

Or barter unwilling
With impassioned clerks after their dues?
I couldn't do with their trade in green
Faceted pineapples which grow slower
Than babies; a season of watching, a shilling.

They cannot raise the time in hut
Or field or tiny hillside patch
To make this petty cash flesh out
Their hard subsistence ways;
So do they walk
To taste the smell of cars

Or marvel why I bargain when my watch
And race betray the farce;
To suck at cans of Coke like men?
And ferment nightly with these yeasts
Their hum-drum round hut small beer feasts.

Bob Windsor   1987

A BREATH OF NIGHT AIR

She struggles to rewind her shawl, made
self-conscious by the stares of tanned
and younger strollers; tries to freeze
herself in shadow. Suddenly ill at ease –

forgetting every inch of flesh displayed
each morning on the neutral sand,
the swaying stride out to the sea,
testing its coldness with her nudity,

and then the basking casual as a seal
on distant rocks; and clearly scarred:
boasting age impartially
as the pale ringed torso of a tree –

Sun blinds her, but these lanterns do not feel
so reassuring. Thrown off guard,
she totters, and in the evening's breeze
modestly pulls her skirt around her knees.

Caroline Price   1991

AT MRS WHITTAKER'S CANAL STREET

Although occasionally house flies
Harbour in the counter display case,
Between the machined cream pies, meat pies,
The industrial Swiss rolls that face
Tea-cakes rivetted with currants; there.
Around eleven, if you call you'll
Get a fried bacon sandwich. It's where
You wait for your cup of tea to cool
Sitting on a sack of potatoes.

Yesterday I saw this woman. Such
A lumpy jumperful, like swedes; nose
Gross as a twisted carrot; not much
Hair, scalp parsnip bare. She was holding
This exquisite cabbage from the net
Of sprout tops. Dark, bossed green enfolding
Frilled emerald. How I did covet
That vegetable treasure, neat-leaved
As any cathedral rose window.

Oh, most glorious green flower
Scattered with the drops of crystal;
Cut from the wide gardens under
January dawns of amber,

And, sometimes,
A grey pearl sadness.

Emma Gleadall   1983

PURDAH

We only want what's best for men.
They are at risk, you know, from the prying
Eyes, or worse, from women who can't be
Trusted to control their lust.

Confronted by the broad planks of a youthful chest
More than suggested by a well-cut shirt or
The round firmnesses of buttocks on a bicycle
Their wanton fingers itch for relief.

For their own freedom and safety, let's
Get those manly limbs enshrouded.
Black is best and watch those ankles
Or even the sun might be tempted.

And something there is in men's hair
That is scandalous; those black curly
Question marks caressing the nape of
The neck are pure provocation.

And pouting lips with perfect teeth
Spell pure damnation. The stubbled jaw
And almond eyes; a road for the lascivious
Tongue, leading straight to perdition.

To save us all, let's keep men hidden
So women's lust can't rise unbidden.

Victoria Field   1998

I'VE ALWAYS WANTED A COWBOY

I've always wanted a cowboy,
with a thick moustache and buckskin gloves.
Along he'd come on his feisty mustang,
just as the sun was setting, just in time,
and he'd scoop me up like a bundle of clothes from the road.
A flurry of hooves, his leather chaps flapping,
and away we'd go.

I'd be startled at first, but I'd cover it well,
wouldn't wince at the bitter coffee he offered
when we stopped to camp for the night,
wouldn't shudder at the howling of wolves,
and when he peeled off his shirt to shake
out the dust, I wouldn't snigger at his high-buttoned long johns.
He'd spread out a blanket, build a small fire,
kick off his stovepipe boots.

High above us, in a curve of prairie dark,
a sliver of moon would flirt with the stars,
and the cowboy would lay aside
his Colt 45 to croon me a song.
His voice would be applewood sweet,
warm with the afterglow of a day, a week, on the road.

Nearby, his horse would snuffle in the moonlight,
nibbling at the grass, and the cowboy
would lower his Stetson to turn the world dark.
'Tomorrow'll be a long day, pretty lady,' he'd say. 'Best rest up.'
But I wouldn't.
Instead, I'd snake myself close like an Indian brave,
summon the cunning of the entire Sioux nation to teach my fingers
a way inside
those high-buttoned long johns.
I'd take my cowboy by surprise.

Virginia Warbey   1997

SOMETHING AUNT ROSIE SAID

'Our lads never got a look-in
after the Yanks came. You
were nearly a G I baby
in my opinion, but never tell
your mother I said so.

I remember, night after hot night,
trying to listen from the window
while they cuddled in our shed,
and did things I couldn't make out
at the time: and some of their names,
Marty, Darren, Wayneford,
B J Stevenson the Third.

Our Mam, she said it was
the nylons, instruments of sin,
that those that give them
think they have the right...

I was too young for more
than chewing-gum, but I
could feel their – I dunno –
their hugeness, all the space
that each one carried around him,
colossal magnetic fields, charisma
we'd call it now, pzazz, you'll
be okay with us babe
the winning team.

Sometimes, afterwards, she'd
whisper me from her bed
and tell me things.
Oh bliss, she'd say, it's all
such bliss. I try to think
about them Rosie, out there,
our boys, and she'd fling her arm out
showing me the sky, but Rosie, Rosie
it's all such fun, and Rosie
darling, you've seen nothing
till you've seen a Yankee soldier
loading up his gun.'

Frances Nagle   1992

MY HUSBAND'S HANDS

I screamed the first time I felt them
freezing, from behind, they seized my wrist
and as he swung my body round the rink
his eyes and blades laughed in electric light.
I knew he liked me then.

In the murmuring dark of Streisand's
　Memories
I sighed when he released my hand
to pass across my shoulders his arm's weight
and trickle down a finger on my throat.
But I knew he liked me.

When he walked me home, and we stood
in the door's shadow and his palms
pressed my back and pulled me to his groin
and his fingers climbed my spine,
I knew.

When we left the church and danced,
and laughed into each other's eyes
and his tongue sucked in my mouth
in front of all those people
I knew how it would be,
alone in our two weeks of sun.

Then, in the happy hour, I planned for babies:
he pretended shock – A football team, I said.
His forearm shook and he capsized
the cocktail I had bought him for a laugh.
The ice sat on his lap, the parasol
red, blue and white – a rosette upon
his darkened crotch. I joked –
He hasn't won his prizes yet – first
we have to pass the litmus test: we don't know
if he'll take …

His eyes were chips of sky above his smile,
but, after, we canoodled in the lift,
tried to look unmarried for the spice
hid our ringed hands inside each other's
    clothes.
Up in our room I turned my head away to dim the
    light.

I managed a half scream inside the flash
of his knee stabbing in my groin
it smashed me into air
onto my toes' tips, against the wall.
His hand, throat-clutching, cut into my
    shock
branded a bruised collar on my skin.
I tried to swallow and to breathe.
He beat his other fist against my ribs, then
in the gasping silence, turned his back.

I tried to breathe, to stand. His knuckles lifted me
towards the bed. Half on the floor he climbed
    astride my hips
sunk nails into my jaw bent back my head. He bit
    into my neck
swore at my whimper and then said
he would be fucked if he would let
a wife of his dictate how he behaved
and it was time I saw my fucking place.
And then he showed me.

Afterwards he stared into my eyes, then wept,
asked me to forgive, it was the drink, the
    cocktail
he was used to beer. I should not have bought it,
never made that joke. On his mother's eyes
this was the last, he'd never lift a hand again,
just please oh please just hold him for tonight.

I always liked his mother,
though I thought she was
a quiet woman.

Margret Christie   1996

NOT QUEEN BUT PAWN

God and the judge
have waved their wands
and I who thought
I came as victim

am now in the dock.
The very fact I walk
in open toed sandals
and clean my teeth

and comb my hair
and cover up
that unattractive wart
is evidence against me.

The meanest shade of eye shadow
is my fault. I
should of course go round
in sackcloth and ashes

whatever that is
or maybe
with my breast cut off
but if I did

I could be blamed
for my unfortunate rapist
relieving himself
with a pig or a dog.

'Women are not the same as men.'*
No. We're the lure
that brings the hawk
penis in. We're carriers

of sexual responsibility
and live in mortal
not venial sin
according to men.

They say since Eve
they never know
which way we'll flow.
We've achieved

the reputation
of sexual slurry.
We're lucky I suppose
that men are predictable,

a good bunk-up
and snore it off
while sentencing us to life
as sluts.

Jenny Hamlett   1992

* Judge Raymond Dean: 'Women are not the same as men. When women say no they don't always mean no. Men can't turn their emotions on and off like a tap as some women can.'

REBOUND
'You've seen a naked man before?' His hand
strokes the stone of my back while I stare
at my bottom drawer (still hanging open
despite the cowboy attempts to ram it shut). Lots
of odds and
sods, and Mike's label of first boyfriend survived him,
John unopened, old soap now, and David,
awkward as a bulky jumper. He is under my skin
while this man slides off it – I
had rather be a welcome mat than a doormat –
body slides open like a banana skin and one man
is far too close for comfort,
and one is far too far away.

Anna Woodford   1999

ELECTRICAL IMPULSES
in the heart, when irregular, are a sign of normality

In bed, embedded, stethoscoped,
so one heart caught the other's race,
out-rivalling your random pace,
I beating wildly, wildly hoped

that you, like me, could not return
to even flow, but now I learn

that hearts take chaos as their norm.
I was deceived by turbulence,
electrified by violence,
to find it signalled calm, not storm.

Barbara Daniels   1997

FOR JANE

What I like in Jane Austen
is when the heroine says,
Are you making love to me, Mr Knightley?
O tempora, o mores.
Nowadays one would think she need hardly ask.

So there I was, phoning you at work
and, my small speech well rehearsed,
prepared to make passionate love to you.
Ten pence in the slot and there you were,
but strange, at once abrupt and neutral.

It was only after several confused moments
– I am easily confused –
I realised I was talking to
or being talked to
or trying to make love to
or being made love to by,
a recorded message.

Not an answering service
(just as well: I was hardly going to go into my act,
spill the beans,
for the benefit of the entire typing pool)
just a brief informative message.

But it was you, your voice
and every bit as precious and as potent to me
as those fading photographs of nearest and dearest
we carry next to our money,
not so secular icons,
the heart's hard currency.

And, listening to you,
apologising, explaining, advising,
I came, that is, to understand
how the sound of words has meaning beyond meaning,
how, when words fail,
begin new ways of our connecting,
language more tender, more telling and true.

In this way, cheap at the price,
you hardly knew it, sweet automaton
– ingenuous in your way as Emma –
we made love half a dozen times.

Eric Jones   1987

WEB

All night, it seemed
She watched the moon slip behind cloud-drifts
And listened
To the soft wave-surge of his breathing.

Next day she came down
Barefoot into the kitchen
And found a spider had slung its web
From doortop to cooker to fridge,
Hair, slighter than breath,
Bringing, strangely,
The wrought lace of grey wedding-veils to mind
Or old shrouds, torn.

She wouldn't break it.
He laughed as she
Clutching her dressing-gown to hide her nakedness
Stooped under it
And she, with the web between them
Laughed back to him.
When he crawled to her
The web shivered
And the bobbed spider gathered itself in.
They whispered
As if the web's spell held them breath-bound

And then it snapped.
Strands swung and drifted, stretched and gave
And the spider ate up what was left
Simply unstitched the long night's work
Hauled itself to earth
And danced to a day-hole.

Untrapped, they watched each other
Possess the space again
And then
As she'd known
He
Stood arm-propped against the door
Watching the drift of rain on roofs
And said
I'm leaving now
And, yes, she said, I knew.

Berlie Doherty   1987

RYDAL WATER

Just as, looking down from Nab Scar, hot and parched
from off the fells, to see it glistening below
and thinking how the best thing in the world
would be to slide into its depths – I thought how
yesterday as she was leaving, she seemed
cool and distant, eager to be gone.
Then wading in, the water brown not blue, chill
and weedy, silt stinking underfoot, a thread-worm
on the surface, enough to kill off all desire
and make one gaze instead at the breeze blown
fastness of Nab Scar – just so tomorrow
hearing what all weekend I dream she'd say,
she'll say it, and that second I'll seem cool
and distant, be only half inclined to stay.

John Sewell   1991

COW

I watch
the calf curve his neck up
and lift a long tongue
curled to the udder.
The cow stands
halted
closes her eyes
slowly
like a woman caressed.

I feel
the calf's long pulling
contract hard
between navel and cervix
recall
when Rosie cried out
hungry
spasms soaked my dress
with sweet spilled milk
the stillness
of my breast in her mouth
her small tongue pulling.

Then I wore my dress loose
to slip easy
with my mother's tongue
I licked her hands clean
bit her soft nails short.
Remembered
how my Grandmother
with my head held firm
licked the lash
out of my stinging eye.

The cow waits
wary at my watching
wipes a green tongue
round her calf's milky mouth
begins to chew again.

Now my dress is fastened tight
my nature dry
folded, neat
like the pure white nightgown
my grandmother kept in a drawer
to be buried in.

Ann Atkinson   1986

HAND WASHING A SMOCK

She immerses her dad's toughened collar,
lets her hands dabble with it.
A few minutes to merge with the window,
the distant, the slagheaps, the water.

She squeezes and lifts the shirt
free of the water,
                      feels some resistance.
Where she has wiped vermilion and cobalt
is stubbornness

and now the grey has gone,
brilliance.
She ventures into the glare of the sun
and shakes the wrung shirt.

Its ripples cascade from father to daughter
and again
from rough struggle between the shoulders
to fine art at her wrists.

Mary Maher   1991

PAVEMENT ARTIST

There are things you never know about parents.
My mother worked at a VD clinic,
her innocence reeling in lost sailors
from the Seamen's Mission in Hope Street.

I see it as a confessional of touch
or double blindfold in which neither
doctor nor patient saw one another.
I expect they were made to flish

the beast around in pink disinfectant
before my mother, thinking of
her histology drawings of
pavement epithelium, Malpighian layers

threaded a *bougie* into the eye of the sore.
Bougie. The word is eponymous
with a town that makes candles in Algeria.
I can see my mother's ghost

wearing a long jellaba and hood
with only her *biro-blue* eyes visible
and weep with her as she lays out
the wax candles of her lost innocence.

Michael Henry   2000

ROUND

It would have been much better
when Roger was dying
on that last day I saw him,
to have knelt,
(impossible by that high hospital steel chrome bed),
to have stood and leaned towards his face
and said, 'I'm sorry to lose you.'
But even then when his body was like a large aquatic mammal
encrusted with sea urchins and barnacles,
we pretended he wasn't actually dying,
not at least in that round.
The nurse lifted him onto a gurney to be weighed
and if you are being weighed
you're still, surely not dead
or going too soon.
His dying felt catching.
The room smelt like a warmed over casserole,
like something cooling.
I held his foot through the blanket
and talked to his friend about her mortgage.
With dimmed eyes I watched him.
For once he was complaining, fevered, incontinent, unwitty.
He comes back to me in dreams
not dead, just well traveled
hoarding rare recordings of Berlioz.

Jill Young   1994

TAKING MARK THIS TIME

I remember you once showing him our photos upstairs.
I couldn't hear his little voice, only yours.
'That's mummy when she was little ... Yes darling,
people do get taller ... Yes, and taller and taller
and taller until one day their heads hit the moon.'

You still look just the same to him in this strange bed.
He gives you a present that he'd hidden from me,
wrapped in silver foil with messy sellotape. He opens it
for you: his favourite car, the one we got him last Christmas
so you could brrmbrrm it along the sheets and get better.

The nurses spoil him while the Asian doctor
takes me to a spare office. For him
I repeat my questions although I know the answers,
like the latest playground riddles. 'Unmentionable,' he says,
when I thank him. I think he means 'Don't mention it.'

I decode your sudden sweat, your shrivelled vowels,
as death buys you off, fills in your O's, sweeps your petals
into heaps, until my cleverness runs out
and you hold your breath as if straining to listen,
a sentry on the red edge of eternity.

He sleeps on the back seat as I chase the night into
the cul-de-sac of dawn, cities closing the distances between them,
one or other claiming every village like young lovers, greedy.
I carry him still sleeping to his bed, his doll eyes
briefly opening. He's only 4, only everything.

Tim Love   1998

CULLING THE HERD

When the new chick flopped
wretched from its shell
(hatched without skin
or the possibility of feathers),
its hen kicked it
to the center of the yard,
plucked at its eyes
and the pecking began.
In the barn, a slant-eyed cat
queened an odd one out,
winkled it from the others
and ate it.

This is how a herd is culled;
the pure and impure separated
to live or die,
each according to its form.

Still, there are exceptions.
The bay mare who dropped
a blind foal and,
not knowing the flaw,
understood that there was one
and bared her teeth
to chase off the herd
then used those molars
to grip its neck
and guide it to her side.

In my own house
a boy child was born
without speech or sound and,
in a hellish lurch,
I recalled the culling
then shoved it off,
rubbed his poor dead ears
and bundled him close
and nursed him.

Jennifer Olds   1993

HAUNTING
To my daughter

When I'm dead, please do try on all my clothes
and ransack all my cupboards. Seek my life.
Don't be the squeamish type, the sort who loathes
to look in secret drawers or use a knife
to prise the locks that guard dark hidden things.
Just say: 'The fraud, she'd want these papers read.
This brooch? I'm going to see what cash it brings
and anyway, she'll never know, she's dead.'
And when, quite unaware, you use my voice,
hear yourself, start, and think yourself possessed,
don't put up a fight, you'll find you have no choice,
I'll often be your uninvited guest.
   Relax, and be content to house my ghost,
   to be my gentle (well-dressed), perfect host.

Janet Loverseed   1997

HOW HE WILL REMEMBER ME

I will be the mean bitch, the witch
shouting rules like incantations,
bat's wing, frog's toe, respect property,
my black garb will obscure
his tantrums, the screaming
hitting, pounding, smashing
of eight-year-old fists and feet
into bathtub porcelain, mirrors,
the skull against the bedroom wall
like a skillful game of chicken.

It will be my coarse voice –
an evil God upon the mountain –
lightning, thunder, commanding
thou shalt not
that he tries desperately to eradicate
raging bile, vomit, diarrhea,
a brew bolder than Hitchcock's birds,
lashing, thrashing as I hold him to the roof:
thou shalt not hurt thyself;
thou shalt not obliterate thy mother.

He will recall my evil nature,
the demagogue, monster, storm
which denied him flight,
an immovable, hated object
when memory serves up
those pre-medicated electric weeks
after Dad had gone to Texas,
long past the endless neglect of a
Korean orphanage where he lay
unfed, undiapered.

Will the calm show through?
Our laughter, giggling, touching,
the fierceness which evaporated
into a mild, if stubborn, boy?
When I am dead
and watching if my soul permits
his growing adult strides,
will he recall the dedication
or abusive preservation
of his life?

Claudette Bass   1995

OVER AND OVER WITH AFFECTION

Seemingly bullet tough.
Though finally
he fell off the bench drunk,
crying for an hour on the floor,
long overdue,
about a friend's death.
Snatched by the drink,
too soon.

While Mick, his new friend
since broken-nose died,
stood over him, drunk too.
Embracing a bottle,
shouting 'get up you fat cunt'
'get up you fat cunt'
over and over with affection.

Jim Lockley   1998

PARTNERS

'Canny good. A fine climb!' you said
as the rock began to blossom with rain.
We packed hurriedly, damp arms stuffed ropes
and bunches of metal into the sacks
as the shower passed.

Down through the dripping conifers,
their smell as strong as petrol,
I recalled you out on the line
whispering nothings for holds.
'It was scary,' you said,
laughter fitted like the car's key.

Driving home we stopped for a pee.
'I was nearly off y'know.'
Our warmth exposed,
steam rose toward the crescent moon.

Bob Cooper   1992

THE ROBERTS

When you find a couple carved in stone,
Like quarrelled sleeping lovers stiffly separate,
You marvel at such permanence of pairing –
Conceive a fiction for the absent flesh:

Four hundred years ago those four eyes wept,
That tense hand touched where stone-folds dip ...
Now, blind slits with tarnished flaps in waiting doorways
Receive delivery of decrees made absolute.

Where will they look, four hundred years from now,
Lovers who need touchstones for their knot?
Already, on a thousand shelves, their reference stands,
Hidden in the DNB Supplement.

Researching a minor painter, they will check
The cumulative index, and find
'MacBryde, Robert. See under Colquhoun',
And turn – to a stormy marriage, solemnized in print.

Anyone who saw the Roberts brawl
(in whatever pub or club or room, whatever time),
who remembers one Lenten face, charcoal drawn,
The other, brush-stroked rubicund and shouting,

Might startle at such authorised avowal
Of indissolubility in men:
Learning that 'the Roberts' after meeting
'Became tender and inseparable companions'.

That was in the beginning, before the drink,
The start of thirty years' monopoly; and now,
As churches have carved couples, brides and grooms,
So libraries house two lovers: MacBryde, Colquhoun.

Paddy Kitchen   1988

SUNDAY SCHOOL OUTING
TO THE BLUEBELL WOODS

Just an old wood and the usual warnings
and lugging the picnics, put you off guard,

unprepared for the world upside down,
that first glimpse of sky on the ground.

More than anything else you wanted to scoop
up all that blueness, to take the shock home.

But when you splashed in, it paled, became
just ordinary flowers, till you learned

the trick was to pick them keeping an eye
on the distance, a kind of horizon to steer by.

And there was something fishy about
how their stems slipped through your fingers,

oozed stickiness – at last slid out,
naked and white, like something owned up to.

Much later, after the leap-frog, the rounders
and biscuits, you all straggled back

down a path trampled with flowers – triumphal
arrived at the bus, where you sat on the lap

of a big girl who'd suddenly picked you
who played with your plaits. Who kissed you.

Back home you rushed in to your mother
your limp armfuls of flowers reburnished

with this new shock. And for nights after
you'd lie awake, deliciously risking

your worst nightmare – you were an orphan,
she was your mother, she'd have to bath you.

Frances Wilson   1993

PORTRAIT AFTER KANDINSKY

Dear aunt of mine whom I have known so long
   I only now see, now we are removed,
the oddness, oddity from where I stand, of you.

The parts, in golden section, of your soul;
   the smaller shaded in bright sun, deep blue
hanging out a painted patterned shield

across your space, to keep away the world.
   Your moonlit section, muted, yet with pink
yellow and white minarets; brown sky but warm

jagged irregular steps. Some worrying things
   a horizon broken at night, not day
a purple head of garlic over all:

and a vertical pink finger, hybrid of,
   forgive, my dear, a condom and a sponge
biscuit with a sugar coating, (ratafia?).

What turmoil, my childhood protector and beacon
   brought you to need to warn the devil off?
Did demons disrupt the balance of your days?

A nephew long removed will never know
   what strangers thronged the mansions of your soul
or how you, the family celibate for whom

the pale pink finger remained, we think, a shadow,
   lived with sharp chaos, quick bright mind
behind that sunlit shield you showed the world.

Moonlit or sunlit, the golden sections join,
   the great arc of your person unites them all.
Dear aunt, would I could say this face to face!

John Ringrose   1999

MEAT

She has her first fall at Christmas.
It's while she's ironing, and she remembers it because
the ironing-board falls on the phone,
cracks the mouthpiece. Inside
she finds a wasp, coiled in the nest of wiring.
Yellow as a high-voltage warning.
Pressed in through the holes
to sleep. She holds it in her hand,
closes the hand into a fist.
It helps her concentrate.

She buys offcuts
and cuts them small,
breakfast, dinner and tea. That way
she gets to watch the box and eat
without missing the action.
But cutting's getting difficult.
She uses kitchen scissors first,
to snicker through the raw meat.

Small things go wrong
whenever they can. It's not senility,
the toilet tap left choking
hot water in the dark, the washing
piling up like nasty thoughts.
Stuff gets lost, capsules especially.
It's just that she's got other things
to think about. One other thing.

King's Cross. Mice wince
between the tracks. She leans against a tube-map, listens
for four-letter words, watches
a pregnant woman sitting down. Bitch,
the bitch. She holds in pain
like mouthfuls of paraffin.

Locks her teeth. If she gives in
it will escape her lips in a cackle
of laughter, then ignite. No one moves.
It knuckles up into a gout. No one
takes the first step. Headphones hiss.
There is a watchtick in her skull,
a fuse burning to reach its dynamite.

Tobias Hill   1995

FALLEN FRUIT

Your blue-gray eyes looked straight into my heart.
I loved your Irish jokes, your mental vigour.
Once met, you could not winkle us apart,
it felt so right for us to live together.
Your blue-gray eyes looked straight into my heart.

Our friends all said we made the perfect couple.
We both were fans of Betjeman and Larkin.
We liked long walks and Stately Homes and Scrabble
and loved our roses and our kitchen garden.
Our friends all said we made the perfect couple.

It was great joy to find a tender lover
when not exactly old, but still not young.
And what we learnt when we embraced each other
was that the tempo changed, but not the song.
It was great joy to find a tender lover.

I had not dreamed that men like you fall ill.
You were so strong. So marvellously alive.
I never thought that you were only mortal
so at the end, my dear, I was not brave.
I had not dreamed that men like you fall ill.

But how I wish you'd taken me to church
before you went to glorify your Maker.
That oversight has left me in the lurch
without the means to pay the Undertaker.
You *should*, you know, have taken me to church!

Ursula Kiernan   1998

DANCING ATTENDANCE
For my mother

She always danced me at weddings. In time,
the upright gave way to the portable,
vampers to LPs and stacked forty-fives.
A last go at Vimto dregs came between
lace hanky lick-wash and hair re-parting.
'Poor lamb's feet!' tangled with the table-lip;
but soon, I sat on the crook of her arm,
loved, never suffered then, the straightening
tie. Once, we took the floor to a big band.
She led on the up beat, quick-stepping in.
Folk we bumped into showed their gratitude:
'Pleased to meet!' Trumpets and saxophones
played to the gallery, bowed as we passed:
Joe Loss to the life unleashed his baton.

Now, swing and spin involves the Mecalift.*
Slings, chains, warning labels bear the legend;
LOAD NOT EXCEEDING TWENTY STONES. She makes
light of fabled welfare measures, steps hard
to take. My dead weight re-jigged jitter-bugs
from bed, to bath, to wheelchair. Her caring
plenty beats the hell out of lifting gear,
proves each turn of the screw more than basic
mechanical principle. Through the hoist's
cutting-in, we remain fair movers, strut
our low-technology stuff. Neat footwork
applied to this form of transport sweeps us
both over thresholds – however loudly
I choose to claim scooting prohibited.

Keith Ashton   1988

---

* Mecalift: a hand-cranked hoist on wheels.

SOME THINGS THAT GO TO MAKE A GOLDEN WEDDING

Dad leaves the bathroom cupboard door ajar.
Mum fills the kitchen sink with too much hot.
Though neither one could fancy caviare,
they'd manage tinned red salmon like a shot.
He wolfs the better half, egg-custard-wise.
Vinegared chitterlings she alone devours.
He pumps her tyres. She cuts his fingernails.
     They kind of compromise
on sport and soaps, and lie together hours
sun-worshipping. Companionship prevails.

He cultivates new shoots from home-grown seed.
She tops and tails the produce, kidney beans.
What nurtures each according to their need
as often keeps the neighbours in free greens.
Stakes in a dream home leave them unimpressed.
The goods they've learned to value don't divide.
No hint of, *who bought what*, or, *growing bored*,
     spoils fifty years possessed.
Enchantment's wealth and tenor coincide.
He sings, Because You're Mine. She smiles, adored.

Keith Ashton   1996

THE MIDGES

I walked the autumn woods alone
where, desperately assembled,
in shafts of dusty brilliance thrown
by sunlight through the beeches' crown,
a few last midges trembled.

The force that set them weaving there
that day in late September
their frantic patterns on the air
had led me to the woodlands where
we'd walked and to remember.

In their compulsive, frenzied dance
you saw our own fate mirrored,
welcomed the happy circumstance
that held us, hapless, in its trance,
to each other quite delivered.

For us, for them, there was no choice,
our fate their fate resembled,
we could not disobey the voice
that told us, while there's chance, rejoice –
(so desperately assembled).

Alone, I walk the woods anew
and see the seasons flying:
spring-summer-autumn, winter too,
but oh, my love, my love for you,
unlike the midges' dance we knew,
takes such a time a-dying.

James Brockway   1993

THIN AIR

Now's the time to close windows
before the wind, already up,
rattles my sleep. I lean
toward me over the sill,
all breasts and flesh fixed orange
in the stare of porch lights.

Night currents shoulder through.
Aniseed. Nettles. Wet earth.
I catch myself deep breathing skin,
holding perfume in. Moths.
Sheep sounds. Somewhere an owl.
Somewhere, growing small, your car.

Diana Syder   1992

ONE FLESH

'She was all woman, all women to me.'
This, after we'd washed her at the hospital, and she'd pleaded
to come home, though he hadn't made a ramp
for her wheelchair yet, and she couldn't get her false teeth in
to eat, her gums jumping all over with the crab
that had settled itself all over.

'I'm going to die tonight,' she'd said, as he held her from behind
for comfort. He held the tea-cup to her lips and countered
'Don't be daft.' 'I am, I am,' she whispered.
He called to tell me in the morning.

I'd thought my parents' marriage
the usual pain, rocking on
through years of compromise and waste.
The flowers he brought her home from work,
his kiss as she leant against the oven
I thought an obligation

I wasn't ready for his 'She was all woman, all women to me':
my needful, salutary exclusion from their marriage.

Julia Casterton   1999

IN G MAJOR

Bach? he wondered, rain
pelting against the windscreen,
sheep clotting the field.

For a minute he envied
their simplicity of choice –
that sense of unresurrected
reality, absence of analysis,
not having to think of the dying.
                    Nothing
phlegmatic about those months…
each one a deep, riving slash
into expectation; the one red-raw
still, un-stitchable, un-healing…

He watched the distant hedgerows
coruscate through the fluid windscreen
like a water-colour wash blipping
on dry *not-pressed*. Thought
of his washes of Tintern and Chepstow
on lost days, her at his side.

'Let's go,' he said to the dog.
'Let's go and get wet.'

Flute Concerto in G Major the voice said.
He did not get the composer's name.
Somehow, it did not matter.

He wanted to hear the drums.

Huw Watkins   1999

DEAR SECOND BED DOWN

may I, as Consultant in the case,
spare a precious second or so
to say what a pleasure it is
finally to allow you Graduation Status.
Your performance in all departments of the cure
has been nothing short of magnificent.
You have responded to the chemotherapy
superbly, as we hoped you would.
Wisp by wisp your hair is returning.
You have dieted, visualised, vindicated
our somewhat tentative hormone programme.
Your blood is beginning to redden up;
your X-rays are stunningly clear.

It is with God's own pleasure I hang
this medal round your neck.

Now go and die of something else.

Geoffrey Holloway   1993

YOUR COUNTRY

You've written about it for years, guessing
the terrain, climate, population, putting
off your journey twice at least, pressing
for more time to question your footing,
destination, welcome by distant relatives
whose tug sometimes felt too compelling.

Last week, after the lousiest of nights,
just before I woke, I saw your smile, telling
me not to fret, to set my life to rights,
return your passport, pissbottle, sedatives.
When I'm sick of this place you'll show me how
the border opens. It's your country now
and though I'd love to see you sound, fit,
I'll do my utmost to postpone my visit.

Patricia Pogson   2000

CRYPT

The first examination of conscience

There are bones
haunting the fridge
with mould on them like moss.
How many years now
since my carnivore days
when I picked the cage
of a chicken carcase clean?
Oh, and that pig's head
that I boiled for brawn
in a Scottish winter.
Remember how I needed
a brick to lid down the snout
when the boiling made the gristle
rear right up with the heat?
The brawn was clear and lovely
like a cache of garnet and pearls.
Never again, though. Never again.

The second examination of conscience

Eggs in a bucket
swimming in isinglass.
Whole eggs from the hens
the shells gone leathery as turtles',
whites gone all to water
yolk sacs slack and milky
so easily torn.
How I cashed in on their
mother-frenzy, my lovely
Rhode Island Red
Light Sussex cross
layers. From point of lay
to their moulting each Nov-
ember I forced them to be
egg-crazy, egg-a-day
wonders. I laid up
their overplus, stashed eggs
like oval ghosts in a pool
against their bald eclipse.

And all infertile, since
I'd *coq-au-vined* long since
their solo cock of the coop.
Never again. I'll not
swallow any of that.
I have no stomach for it.

The third examination of conscience

When I bought the cleaver
at the butcher's suppliers
in the cold hinterland of East Kilbride
the man behind the counter
asked me quite straight
did I get on, like,
with my old man?
      Fine.
Oh, I knew then fine
what cleaving was:
to split with a blow
or to hold on tight.
A man and a woman
shall be one flesh.
Cleave thou only
unto him. One flesh.

Catherine Byron 1999

PRAYER

Mandrax, Mogadon, Largactil and Librium,
soften the bed where I seek oblivion.
If I should surface before I succumb,
may your embraces keep me strong.

Eamer O'Keeffe 1995

FAT SHADOW

Bulimia Nervosa

I
Out of the squat mid-day shadows
that spread even from anorectics,
a butterfly, marbled white, soars,
dips, hovers, on a trick-kite
flight-path to the kiss and promise
of nettle-flower after nettle-flower.
Pale dusted wings ghost the black
silk-thread skeleton; but catching
a coarser light, the delicate glutton
thickens to curds veined with mould.

II
Seen only in fasts between feasts,
purged flesh is lean, but the fat
shadow must be dragged from sight
and fed: jaws stretched sobbing,
gobbling until crammed bellyful
of slop and sugar infant junkets,
or gulletted with half-chewed gobbets
from grease and grunt banquets,
or pelican-pouched, brimming chocful
from one cream-whipped swallowing binge.

III
The gorge rises, churned sour
in the sickness of rejection, to retch
and void, before the water sluices,
harsh, cold, to wash, wash, until
the gut aches. For a while the wasting
satisfies, the emptiness bites acrid
as cigarette smoke, brittle as the cough.
But the poison holds, grip slackened
with laxative, jolted by emetic,
yet never quite flushed out.

IV
After the vomit has been sponged and swabbed,
a fresh hunger begs to be staled,
sated, by an excess of salt-skinned
lovers, each to be heaved away,
the short-lived drench in syrup
forgotten. Sharing in the final
swollen intrusion if you savour
only the act of consumption, wanting
to be clean as a scraped bone, wanting
more to be eaten than to eat.

David Duncombe   1991

SKINNING THE BULL

We haul the carcass up to a beam,
sailors tugging a black sail

twisting round in the barn's gale,
while the knife shines in the gloom

the head is cut off in a cloud of steam
guts flower geranium

and the skin drops in a crumpled heap,
a highwayman's cloak,

while he kneels and strokes
into the flesh, bone by bone

till the body swings open
like coming home.

John Daniel   2000

LEADING MARIGOLD TO THE BULL

In a misty fluorescence,
a humid fade of rain,

all day was tingling. Evening,
silver-willowed, damp umbellifers,

we went down the lane
with her wood-creak hoofs
on tarmac.

How the sudden blare of her need
fog-horned the hedges,

beautiful, beautiful, it cried,
release from suffering.

I wanted to lead all men
to women, all women to men,

where their blood blared
lonely, unheard,

and their breath warmed on the rope,
loosing at the gate.

Beautiful, beautiful, they wait.

Chris Maudsley   1998

DOG

Smell in a dog's fur is the dear
guilty odour of trust; for dog
of my earlier days was my rival
                as I was his.

Him I pissed upon. When he died,
Grandmother keened with a will. Stoic
of eight years' standing I made strict
                silence suffice.

Dog of my changing years was chosen
friend. Him I would serve selflessly
striding straight into a frozen
                Dee after him

when, innocent pup, he broke ice;
stanching the blood, bearing him home
when, grown galumpher on the moor,
                he trod cracked glass.

He it was who on the same moor seized
by a fit and caressed over it
baptized my hand, like Cowper's hare,
                with gratitude.

Why will some seek out dogs, you ask,
for trust's giving and receiving?
Amid treacheries they cling to
                trust doggedly.

William Imray   1989

ROAD KILL:
ON SEEING A DEAD CAT FREED FROM WINTER'S ICY GRIP

A spring afternoon, cool sun upon my back,
hardly has the roadside snow begun to melt,
on a low bough of a roadside tree three crows,
glossy blue-black against the blue-white sky,
bob heads in silent conversation and watch
for signs of life in a small, grey, tabby
cat that lies, curled on a cushion of hard
packed snow. The warming sun has melted away
all but the snow underneath the cat and now
it rests, lips curled from white teeth, eyes wide,
ears pricked, but yet un-warmed from its icy
sleep of wintry death, upon its white pedestal
of ice sculptured by sun and wind, tail twisted
over body, one back leg splayed as though
to rise; – a marble pet at the cold, stone
armoured feet of a medieval knight, five hundred
years upon his snow white marble sarcophagus
in a cold and silent church.
    A feral cat, seeking field mice in the snowy
ditch, right by the tree's drift of snow, too
intent perhaps on catching a burrowing mouse, or
deafened by a winter gale, failing to hear
the snow plough's snow-muffled approach, got
buried under an avalanche of hard, packed snow
and, fatigued with many efforts to free itself,
had curled up in the tomb it made, to wait out
the winter, sleeping.
    The crows carry on their lively argument, but
there's no movement from the cat, no carrion odour
rises from its deep frozen blood to stir their
appetites and soon they give up their vigil to glide
silently as mourners leaving a wintry churchyard,
to search the road sides for more lively road-kill.

Michael-J Bakerpearce   1998

CONTRIBUTORS

Keith Ashton Lived in Lincoln. He was born with muscular dystrophy (1951) and never walked. He graduated from Reading University in 1975 with Honours in Fine Art. His poetry collection *Fair Moving* is still available from Arc Publications.

Ann Atkinson Has an MA in Contemporary Poetry. Poems in *PN Review, New Welsh Review, Writing Women, The Nerve* (Virago) 1998 and *Beginnings* (The Housman Society anthology) 2000. Is looking forward to a few years of co-editing Staple – though maybe not 20!

Michael-J Bakerpearce Bred in Derbyshire but after returning to Britain from India post-war became resident in Canada. Widely published. Says no-one in his family understands his poetry.

Elizabeth Barrett Born in Sheffield 1961. First degree and PhD at the University of London before returning to Sheffield in 1994 where she lives with her husband and two children. Co-editor Staple from July.

Claudette Bass Lived with her son in California at the time of the poem. She writes: 'Ethan is a brilliant and handsome young man of nearly 16, but remains emotionally ill. (He was institutionalized in December 2000 for trying to kill me yet again.)'

Roy Blackman Lives in Suffolk where he co-edits the poetry magazine *Smiths Knoll* and is secretary to the Aldeburgh Poetry Trust Committee. His first collection *As Lords Expected* (not about cricket) appeared with Rockingham in 1996.

James Brockway Died recently. He had a long career as a writer and translator in Holland. Very widely published. Knight of the Order of the Lion of the Netherlands.

Philip Brown Studied Classics, became an English teacher, took early retirement: is a member of the Gloucestershire folk/poetry group, Holub Poets. Work in various magazines and anthologies.

Pat Buik Is matriarch of a large, scattered tribe. She enjoys celebrations, growing things and writing poems. Her work has appeared widely; from *The Countryman* to *The London Magazine*.

Catherine Byron Grew up in Belfast, farmed in Scotland, and now teaches at the Nottingham Trent University. Working towards a joint exhibition of texts on vellum and glass with Dublin artist Denis Brown. Her fifth collection, *The Getting Of Vellum*, is co-published by Salmon and Blackwater, (2000).

Victor Callaghan Perhaps Staple's least aspirant contributor. Wrote nothing till aged 60, after Navy, Oxford, teaching.

Peter Cash Born in Lincolnshire, educated at Nottingham University, he has now been Head of English Studies at Newcastle-under-Lyme School in Staffordshire for sixteen years. His fourth collection *Fen Poems* was a Staple FIRST EDITION.

Julia Casterton Author of *Creative Writing A Practical Guide* (Macmillan) 1986 and 1998 and three collections of poetry. Teaches for the Open University, University of North London and City Lit.

Margret Christie Lives in Derbyshire with two cats, two dogs, one husband and at least three jobs. Trying to keep up.

Paul Christmas Has been published widely and won several competitions. Has appeared on Welsh television and Radio 4 Kaleidoscope as part of the Border Poets Project. Now living and working in Hereford.

Bob Cooper A rock climber and clergy person, last heard of in Warrington. Poems have appeared in climbing and poetry magazines here and in the USA.

John Daniel Lives in Totnes, Devon. Winner of the Exeter Poetry prize 1995, published in Faber *Introduction* series.

Barbara Daniels Started writing poetry late in life; her poems have appeared widely and several have won prizes in competitions. She has three books published by the National Poetry Foundation: *Dance With Me, Spin Again* and *Mean Time*.

Michael Daugherty Is a widely published poet underground and overground. Amateur ornithologist, ex-rockclimber, potholer, sometime executive whiz-kid, civil servant, steelcutter, shop manager, professional gambler, political activist, dream-traveller. Still Manx.

Berlie Doherty Lives in the Peak District. Author of a number of novels for young people. including TV serialisations. In 1987 she was awarded the Carnegie Medal for *Granny Was A Buffer Girl* and for *Dear Nobody* in 1991.

Roshan Doug Born in 1963. Educated at universities of Lancaster and Nottingham. Lectures at the University of Birmingham, and is Tutor at the University of Wolverhampton. Birmingham's Poet Laureate in 2000. Two collections of poems: *Delusions* 1995 and *The English-knowing Men* 1999.

David Duncombe Member of editorial team from Staple 6. Once a school headteacher, he has written two novels for children and radio drama. First prizes in the Yorkshire, Ilkley and Surrey poetry competitions. Collections: *A Brave Show* (Free Man's Press), *Pencilling In* (Redbeck), *Occupational Hazard* (Jackson's Arm).

Roger Elkin Has been editor of *Envoi* since 1992; and his poetry has won many prizes in Poetry Competitions. His second collection *Points Of Reference* (Headland) is available; this poem, *Hill Farmers*, is part of a forthcoming collection *Home Ground* also from Headland.

Richard Epstein Published in many magazines in the US and UK.

Victoria Field Was born in London in 1963. She has lived and worked in Turkey, Russia, Pakistan and Cornwall, as well as in the countries of the imagination.

Emma Gleadall Is still here, still writing and publishing, enjoying life. Has just become a great-grandmother.

Ulf Goebel Is currently teaching English at a college in Brooklyn, New York. He continues scheming for a longer narrative exploring his personal history along fictional lines.

Elizabeth Gowing Studied English at Magdalen College, Oxford. She works as a teacher and educational consultant in London. Poetry and short stories in *Foolscap, Ambit* and Dillons' *May Anthology*, etc.

Sheila Hamilton Is widely published in magazines and has a pamphlet collection forthcoming from Flarestack. She lives with her young family and cat on the Wirral.

Jenny Hamlett Works as a writing teacher for both Link Into Learning and for adult education. Her poems have been published in a variety of magazines and heard on local radio. She has published two children's stories.

June Ella Harris Lives in Devon. Work in small press magazines, etc.

Paul Heapy Lives in Derbyshire. Hoping to make a bit of a comeback with two sets of interlinked poems.

Michael Henry Lives in Cheltenham. He was a runner-up in the 1999 National Poetry Competition. His third collection *Footnote To History* published by Enitharmon Press.

Donna Hilbert *Women Who Make Money And The Men Who Love Them*, Staple FIRST EDITION, 1994. Latest collection is *Transforming Matter* (Pearl Editions) 2000. Pudding House is to publish *Donna Hilbert Greatest Hits 1989-2000*.

Tobias Hill His collection of poetry *Year Of The Dog* won an Eric Gregory award. *Midnight In The City of Clocks* was a PBS Recommendation. His book of stories, *Skin*, won the Pen-Macmillan Prize for Fiction. His novel *Underground* won a British Arts Council award. Faber published his second novel *The Love Of Stones* in February.

Helen Hills Teaches in the Department of Art History at the University of Manchester.

Geoffrey Holloway Was still writing poetry the day before he died. His final collection *And Why Not* was published by Flambard Press in 1997.

William Imray (Brown) Born Aberdeen 1927. Degree in Classics. Senior Lecturer, Aberdeen College of Education 1962-79. Retired early to write verse. Many poems published: two collections. Organist and Choirmaster 1990-97: translation and composition of hymns (words and music). Recently translated *Oresteia* into Scots.

Eric Jones At the time the poem was first published he was living in Liverpool where he nursed the mentally handicapped.

Pauline Keith Firmly re-rooted in the North West after work in the Near and Far East, Nigeria, Holland and Canada. Misses classes such as the one in this poem, but enjoys tutoring occasional Creative Writing groups.

Ursula Kiernan Widely published. Short-listed for the Rosemary Arthur Award in 1999. First collection *Fish That Sing* (NPF) 1999. *Animals With Attitude* (Krax) 2000. Competition prizes include four Firsts. She lives in West Sussex with a Chihuahua dog and two Bengal cats.

Anne Kind Born in Berlin, came to England in 1934. Trained as a nurse. Administrator for FPA, 1954 to 1981, and for LOROS Leicestershire Hospice Care, 1981 to 1987. OBE in Queen's New Year's Honours List 1990. Poetry in *Stand, New Hope International* and in the anthology *Long Pale Corridor* (Bloodaxe) 1996, etc.

Jenny King Her poetry is published widely in magazines. She has a short collection from Mandeville. She is married to a medieval historian and lives in Sheffield where she recently took an MA in contemporary poetry.

Paddy Kitchen Born 1934, she has published a dozen books including a biography of Gerard Manley Hopkins. Still hasn't met Bob Dylan or been to Botswana; but did horseride again after a gap of 47 years.

Jim Lockley Born in Manchester in 1961 – not as dull as it sounds. Lives in Nottingham. Interested in dancing, meditation, Tantra. Works as a community photographer.

Tim Love Lives in Cambridge. His poetry has appeared in *Stand, Rialto, Verse* and various WWW publications.

Janet Loverseed Her poetry is published in a number of magazines. She lives in Stockport, where she has given up work for the lazy and/or more creative life.

Mary Maher She continues to write, give readings and workshops. Last year she gave a reading in Castle Drogo with David Santer which was a particular thrill.

Chris Maudsley Was born in Leeds, and in 1998 was living in Dyfed, single parent. Poetry for Special Needs. Dairy small time. All Ireland first prize Farmhouse Yoghurt 1995.

Berenice Moore Leicester poet. One-time primary teacher. Poems in widely ranging magazines and anthologies. Still writing, still aiming for the heights.

Margaret Moore Born and educated in Northern Ireland. Since 1979 she has lived in Cambridge. A former psychologist and crime writer, she now concentrates on poetry.

Frances Nagle Lives in Marple Bridge, Stockport, where she works in an office. Her collection *Steeplechase Park* is published by Rockingham. Her pamphlet of poems for children *You Can't Call A Hedgehog Hopscotch* is from Dagger Press.

Maggie Norton Poet and story teller, performer of *Tales Of Terror*, broadcaster and writer in education. Two collections of poetry for primary children. Editor of poetry anthology *Swarthmoor*. Poems in *Sunday Times, Smiths Knoll, OU Poets*, etc.

Eamer O'Keeffe Irish-born, based in London. One-time film-maker and subversive cartoonist. Performer with Survivors Poetry. Work in *Angel Exhaust, Boadicea, DAIL, First Time, NHI, Orbis, Psychopoetica, Silver Wolf*, etc.

Jennifer Olds Has graduated and is working for her MA. Two sons growing up fast. Still living in Chino, California, and is about to re-marry.

Geoff Pickering Retired English lecturer. Lives in Derby. Interested in poetry and theology.

Patricia Pogson Her collection *The Tides In The Basin* was published by Flambard Press in 1994. A booklet dedicated to Geoffrey Holloway is with her publishers.

Caroline Price Violinist and teacher living in Kent. Poetry and short stories have appeared widely. Her collection *Pictures Against Skin* published by Rockingham Press. Has run workshops in schools and a men's prison and in 1997 gave readings in Kent and Northern Europe. Working on a commission from Medway District Council.

D A Prince Born in 1947 of Welsh parents in Leicestershire. Her first collection *Undoing Time* was from Pikestaff in 1998. A chapbook (Manifold) is due soon, and a further Pikestaff collection in 2002.

Tony Rees Is a lot more cheerful since he got shot of lecturing at the University of Derby; politically he supports Plaid Cymru; his religion is socialism.

John Ringrose Ex-actor, ex-medical research Appeals Director. Several radio plays broadcast and a biography published by Granada. Founder member of Thameside Poetry Workshop. Poems in various magazines. Lives in Greenwich, and is married, with three daughters, to a community playwright.

Guy Russell Born in 1965 and currently works in the printing industry in Milton Keynes. The full-length *Thatcher In Hell* is a mini-epic with Mrs T as its anti-heroine.

Maurice Rutherford Born in Hull in 1922 and after a working life in the ship-repairing industry retired to Bridlington where he still lives. His poetry volumes include *This Day Dawning* (Peterloo) 1994 and *After The Parade* (Shoestring) 1996.

Hillel Schwartz Lives in California. Poetry widely published in the US, Canada and UK in *Iron*, *Orbis* and *European Judaism*, etc.

John Sewell Lives in Bakewell. Appeared first in Staple 3 and was a sometime editor. Is proud of his 16 year association with the magazine and pleased that it is now more numerically advanced than he is.

Jon Silkin Founder of *Stand* magazine and editor for forty four years. An extraordinary feat.

K V Skene Recently published in UK, US, Australian, Irish and Canadian magazines. Latest book *Elemental Mind* from Broken Jaw Press (Canada). A chapbook due from Hilton House (UK).

Pauline Stainer Lives in Suffolk after three years in the Orkneys. Bloodaxe published *Parable Ireland* in 1999 and will publish her *Selected Poems* next year.

Julian Stannard Work – everywhere! A first book *Rina's War* (Peterloo) due in 2001. Teaches at a constituent college of UEA.

Michael Stone Born in Berlin, he came to England as a 15 year old on the Kinder Transport as part of the Jewish exodus from Nazi Germany. A life-long Marxist he returned to Berlin in 1966 where he worked as a writer and TV critic.

Diana Syder Lives in the Peak District. Poetry books include *Hubble* (Smith Doorstop), *The Blue Bang Theory* (Redbeck) and a pamphlet *Catching The Light* (Slow Dancer). She won the 1996 Poetry Business Competition and was a runner-up in the 1998 Arvon. Recently the Institute of Physics gave her an award for her poetry.

Virginia Warbey Lives in Southampton and has an MA in Creative Writing. She is married to a social worker and works at a local library, often scribbling poems when she should be shelving books.

Roger Waterfield Born in 1932 in India. Read Classics at Cambridge; taught; retired early; lives in mid-Wales. Other involvements and concerns include the Church and the Labour Party.

Huw Watkins Born and grew up in the Rhondda. Has lived in Leicestershire since 1946. One of the six poets published in Staple FIRST EDITION, *Sestet*. *Times* (booklet) was published in 1984. Forthcoming publications by Leafe Press. Now painting (hopefully) and combining, sometimes, with poetry.

Ben Wilensky Lives in New York. Merchant seaman, soldier, news reporter, art teacher. His poems and stories have appeared around the world.

Frances Wilson Writes, paints and teaches in Hertfordshire. Collection *Close To Home* from Rockingham Press. Has subscribed to and enjoyed Staple for over ten years.

Anna Woodford Works at University of Durham. Shortlisted for an Eric Gregory Award and published in *Iota, Iron, Envoi, The North, Magma, The Reater, Smiths Knoll*, etc.

Jill Young Lives in Los Angeles with her husband, son and daughter. Her poetry has appeared in *Pearl, A New Geography Of Poets*, etc.

Staple is much obliged to Ian Davies of Auckland for assistance with computer artwork for the present dust jacket.

Donald Measham, Bill Berrett, Bob Windsor of Staple

Donald Measham and Bob Windsor were founding editors (with Tony Rees) and have worked together on all but one of the last thirty issues. David Duncombe and John Sewell have also for many years been associated with Staple. They co-edited or edited seven issues of the magazine and had an equal share of editorial responsibility for twelve Staple First Edition collections.

Bill Berrett, Staple's designer, brought from his work in Architecture and Planning a conviction that good content needed good presentation to achieve credibility. Professional typesetting, printing and binding were in place by issue 5; the number of each issue providing the basis for its cover design. Thus 6, the New Zealand fern; 8, early eighties post-modernism; 17, a Supermarket bar code; 19, Winter sun... The covers are in groups of ten: teens angular, twenties curvilinear, thirties circular, and forties 'Streamline revival'. Good printing has indulged a taste for colour vibrations at the edges of adjacent bright colours.

In 2001 and after, Staple, which began as stapled sheets with hand-drawn covers (daffodils, suburbia, Miners' strike), will continue to provide an attractive showcase for writers. It plans, too, to reintroduce Staple Writing Days.